THIS BOOK

BELONGS TO

....

Did you like my book? I pondered it severely before releasing this book. Although the response has been overwhelming, it is always pleasing to see, read or hear a new comment. Thank you for reading this and I would love to hear your honest opinion about it. Furthermore, many people are searching for a unique book, and your feedback will help me gather the right books for my reading audience.

Thanks!

TABLE OF CONTENTS

Introduction 27

Chapter 1: Knitting and Purling 29

Chapter 2: Swatches and Squares 35

Chapter 3: Reading Your Patterns 38

Chapter 4: Tips, Tricks and Tools 39

Chapter 5: Simple Stitch Patterns 46

Chapter 6: Slip Stitches 58

Chapter 7: Cables 67

Chapter 8: Lace Patterns 77

Chapter 9: Glossary 91

SUMMARY

The Timeless Art of Knitting: Its Significance and Beauty:

The Timeless Art of Knitting: Its Significance and Beauty is a comprehensive exploration of the rich history, cultural significance, and aesthetic beauty of knitting. This book delves into the origins of knitting, tracing its roots back to ancient civilizations and highlighting its evolution over time.

The author takes readers on a journey through various knitting techniques, from basic stitches to intricate patterns, showcasing the versatility and creativity that can be achieved through this craft. The book also delves into the different types of yarns and fibers used in knitting, providing valuable insights into their characteristics and how they can be best utilized.

One of the key aspects that sets this book apart is its exploration of the cultural significance of knitting. The author delves into the role of knitting in different societies and how it has been used as a means of self-expression, storytelling, and even political activism. Through captivating anecdotes and historical examples, the book highlights the ways in which knitting has been intertwined with social movements and cultural traditions.

Furthermore, The Timeless Art of Knitting: Its Significance and Beauty celebrates the therapeutic benefits of knitting. The author delves into the calming and meditative qualities of this craft, highlighting how it can serve as a form of stress relief and mindfulness practice. The book also explores the sense of accomplishment and pride that comes with creating something by hand, fostering a sense of self-worth and creativity.

In addition to its informative content, this book is visually stunning. It is filled with vibrant photographs showcasing exquisite knitted creations, from intricate lace shawls to cozy sweaters. The detailed step-by-step instructions and diagrams make it accessible to knitters of all skill levels, whether they are beginners or experienced practitioners.

Overall, The Timeless Art of Knitting: Its Significance and Beauty is a must-read for anyone interested in knitting, whether as a hobby or a profession. It offers a comprehensive exploration of the craft's history, cultural significance, and aesthetic beauty, while also providing practical guidance and inspiration. This book is sure to ignite a passion for knitting and leave readers with a deeper appreciation for this timeless art form.

Embarking on Your Knitting Journey: What to Expect:

Knitting is a wonderful and fulfilling hobby that allows you to create beautiful and functional items with just a pair of needles and some yarn. If you are just starting out on your knitting journey, it's important to know what to expect and how to navigate the world of knitting.

First and foremost, it's important to understand that knitting is a skill that takes time and practice to master. Like any new skill, there will be a learning curve, and you may encounter some frustrations along the way. However, with patience and perseverance, you will soon find yourself creating intricate patterns and designs.

When you first start knitting, it's best to begin with simple projects and basic stitches. This will help you build a solid foundation and get comfortable with the mechanics of knitting. Scarves, dishcloths, and simple hats are great projects for beginners. As you gain confidence and skill, you can gradually move on to more complex patterns and techniques.

One of the most important aspects of knitting is choosing the right yarn and needles for your project. Yarn comes in a variety of weights and fibers, each with its own unique characteristics. It's important to consider the pattern you are working on and the desired outcome when selecting your yarn. Needles also come in different sizes and materials, and the size of your needles will determine the gauge and tension of your knitting. It's a good idea to experiment with different yarns and needles to find what works best for you.

As you progress in your knitting journey, you will also learn about different knitting techniques and stitches. Knitting involves a combination of knit and purl stitches, which create different textures and patterns. There are also various techniques for increasing and decreasing stitches, as well as more advanced techniques like cables and lacework. Exploring these techniques will allow you to expand your knitting repertoire and create more intricate and unique projects.

Another important aspect of knitting is understanding knitting patterns. Knitting patterns are like a roadmap for your project, providing instructions on stitch counts, shaping, and finishing details. It's important to read and understand the pattern before you begin, as this will help you avoid mistakes and ensure that your finished project turns out as intended. As you become more experienced, you may even start creating your own patterns and designs.

Knitting is not only a creative outlet, but it also offers numerous benefits for your mental and emotional well-being.

Navigating Through This Comprehensive Guide of Knitting: Welcome to this comprehensive guide on knitting! Whether you are a beginner or an experienced knitter looking to expand your skills, this guide is designed to help you navigate through the world of knitting with ease and confidence.

Knitting is a versatile and creative craft that allows you to create beautiful and functional items using just a pair of needles and some yarn. From cozy scarves and hats to intricate sweaters and blankets, the possibilities are endless. However, if you are new to knitting, it can seem overwhelming at first. That's where this guide comes in.

We will start by covering the basics of knitting, including the different types of needles and yarns available, as well as the essential techniques you need to know. We will explain how to cast on, knit, purl, and bind off, which are the building blocks of knitting. We will also delve into more advanced techniques such as increasing, decreasing, and working with different stitch patterns.

Once you have mastered the basics, we will guide you through various knitting projects, ranging from simple and quick to more complex and time-consuming. We will provide step-by-step instructions, along with helpful tips and tricks, to ensure your success in each project. Whether you want to knit a cozy scarf for yourself or a baby blanket for a loved one, we have got you covered.

In addition to the practical aspects of knitting, we will also explore the creative side of this craft. We will discuss color theory and how to choose the right colors for your projects. We will also explore different types of yarns and their properties, helping you make informed decisions when selecting materials for your projects.

Furthermore, we will delve into the world of knitting patterns. We will explain how to read and interpret knitting patterns, including deciphering abbreviations and understanding pattern repeats. We will also provide guidance on how to modify patterns to suit your preferences and measurements.

Throughout this guide, we will address common challenges and mistakes that knitters often encounter, offering troubleshooting tips and solutions. We understand that knitting can be frustrating at times, but with the right guidance and practice, you will overcome any obstacles and become a confident knitter.

So, whether you are a beginner looking to learn the basics or an experienced knitter seeking inspiration and new techniques, this comprehensive guide is your go-to resource. Get ready to embark on a knitting journey filled with creativity, relaxation, and the satisfaction of creating beautiful handmade items. Let's dive in and start navigating through this comprehensive guide of knitting!

A Brief History and Cultural Significance of Knitting: Knitting is a craft that has been practiced for centuries and holds great cultural significance in many parts of the world. Its origins can be traced back to ancient times, with evidence of knitted items found in archaeological sites dating back to the 11th century. However, it is believed that knitting may have been practiced even earlier, as early as the 3rd century BC.

The exact origins of knitting are still debated among historians, but it is widely accepted that it originated in the Middle East, specifically in Egypt and the Arabian Peninsula. From there, it spread to Europe and other parts of the world through trade routes and cultural exchanges. Knitting was initially a practical skill used to create warm and durable garments, such as socks, hats, and sweaters, to protect against the harsh winters.

In the Middle Ages, knitting became more widespread and gained popularity among both the nobility and the common people. It was during this time that knitting guilds were established, which played a crucial role in the development and preservation of knitting techniques. These guilds provided a platform for knitters to share their knowledge and skills, ensuring that the craft was passed down from generation to generation.

During the Renaissance period, knitting became a fashionable pastime among the upper classes. Knitted garments were adorned with intricate patterns and designs, showcasing the skill and creativity of the knitter. Knitting also became a symbol of wealth and status, as only the wealthy could afford the expensive materials and dedicate the time required to create these elaborate pieces.

In the 19th century, knitting underwent a significant transformation with the invention of the knitting machine. This revolutionized the industry, making it possible to produce knitted items on a larger scale and at a faster pace. As a result, knitting became more accessible to the general population, and the craft began to evolve beyond its utilitarian roots.

Today, knitting continues to be a popular hobby and a form of artistic expression. It is no longer limited to creating functional garments but has expanded to include a wide range of items, such as accessories, home decor, and even sculptures. Knitting communities have formed both online and offline, providing a space for knitters to connect, share patterns, and inspire each other.

The cultural significance of knitting extends beyond its practical and artistic aspects. It is often associated with warmth, comfort, and a sense of home. Knitted items are often passed down through generations, becoming cherished heirlooms that carry memories and stories.

Basic Knitting Terminology and Abbreviations Explained in Detail

Knitting is a popular craft that involves creating fabric by interlocking loops of yarn with knitting needles. If you are new to knitting, it is essential to familiarize yourself with the basic terminology and abbreviations used in knitting patterns and instructions. Understanding these terms will help you follow patterns accurately and create beautiful knitted projects. In this guide, we will provide a comprehensive explanation of the most commonly used knitting terminology and abbreviations.

1. Knit (K): Knitting is the fundamental stitch in knitting. To knit, insert the right-hand needle into the front of the stitch on the left-hand needle, wrap the yarn around the right-hand needle, and pull it through the stitch, creating a new stitch on the right-hand needle. This stitch creates a smooth, v-shaped pattern on the fabric.

2. Purl (P): Purling is the second basic stitch in knitting. To purl, insert the right-hand needle into the front of the stitch on the left-hand needle, but from right to left, wrap the yarn around the right-hand needle, and pull it through the stitch, creating a new stitch on the right-hand needle. This stitch creates a bumpy, horizontal pattern on the fabric.

3. Yarn Over (YO): A yarn over is an increase stitch that creates an extra stitch and a small hole in the fabric. To yarn over, bring the yarn to the front of the work (if it's not already there), then wrap it over the right-hand needle from back to front. This creates a new stitch on the right-hand needle.

4. Slip (Sl): Slipping a stitch means transferring it from the left-hand needle to the right-hand needle without knitting or purling it. To slip a stitch, insert the right-hand needle into the stitch on the left-hand needle as if to purl, but without wrapping the yarn around the needle. Then, simply slide the stitch from the left-hand needle to the right-hand needle.

5. Knit Two Together (K2tog): Knitting two stitches together is a decrease stitch that reduces the number of stitches on the needle. To knit two together, insert the right-hand needle into the next two stitches on the left-hand needle as if to knit, wrap the yarn around the right-hand needle, and pull it through both stitches, creating a new stitch on the right-hand needle.

Types and Characteristics of Yarn and Needles of Knitting:

When it comes to knitting, the choice of yarn and needles plays a crucial role in determining the outcome of your project. Yarn and needles come in various types and have different characteristics, each offering unique advantages and considerations. Understanding these factors will help you make informed decisions and achieve the desired results in your knitting endeavors.

Let's start with yarn. Yarn is the primary material used in knitting and is available in a wide range of fibers, weights, and textures. The type of yarn you choose will depend on the project you have in mind and the desired characteristics of the finished piece.

One of the most common types of yarn is wool. Wool yarn is known for its warmth, elasticity, and durability. It is an excellent choice for knitting garments such as sweaters, hats, and scarves, as it provides insulation and retains its shape well. However, wool can be prone to shrinking and may require special care during washing.

Cotton yarn, on the other hand, is lightweight, breathable, and perfect for knitting summer garments and accessories. It is soft and hypoallergenic, making it suitable for those with sensitive skin. However, cotton yarn lacks the elasticity of wool and may stretch over time, so it is important to consider this when selecting your needles and stitch patterns.

Acrylic yarn is a synthetic option that is widely available and affordable. It is known for its softness, easy care, and wide range of colors. Acrylic yarn is a great choice for beginners as it is forgiving and easy to work with. However, it may not have the same warmth and natural feel as wool or cotton.

Other types of yarn include silk, bamboo, alpaca, and blends of different fibers. Each type has its own unique characteristics, such as sheen, drape, and stitch definition. It is important to consider these factors when selecting yarn for your project, as they will influence the overall look and feel of the finished piece.

Now let's move on to knitting needles. Knitting needles come in various materials, lengths, and sizes, each offering different benefits and considerations.

The most common materials for knitting needles are metal, wood, and plastic. Metal needles, such as aluminum or stainless steel, are durable, smooth, and provide excellent stitch glide. They are great for knitting with slippery yarns and for creating tight stitches.

Assembling Your Essential Knitting Toolkit: When it comes to knitting, having the right tools is essential for a successful and enjoyable experience. Whether you're a beginner or an experienced knitter, having a well-stocked knitting toolkit will ensure that you have everything you need to create beautiful and intricate designs.

First and foremost, you'll need a good set of knitting needles. There are various types of knitting needles available, including straight needles, circular needles, and double-pointed needles. The type of needles you choose will depend on the type of project you're working on. Straight needles are ideal for flat knitting, while circular needles are great for knitting in the round. Double-pointed needles are used for knitting small, circular projects such as socks or hats. It's a good idea to have a range of needle sizes in your toolkit to accommodate different yarn weights and project sizes.

Next, you'll need a selection of yarn. Yarn comes in different weights, which refers to the thickness of the yarn. Common yarn weights include lace, fingering, sport, worsted, and bulky. Each weight is suitable for different types of projects, so it's important to have a variety of yarn weights in your toolkit. Additionally, consider the fiber content of the yarn. Popular options include wool, cotton, acrylic, and blends. Experimenting with different yarns will help you discover your preferences and create unique pieces.

In addition to needles and yarn, you'll need a few other essential tools. A pair of scissors is necessary for cutting yarn, so make sure to have a small, sharp pair in your toolkit. Stitch markers are also useful for marking specific stitches or sections in your knitting. They come in various shapes and sizes, and can be either removable or fixed. Stitch holders or safety pins are handy for holding stitches when you need to set aside a section of your work. A tape measure is essential for checking gauge and measuring your progress. Lastly, a yarn needle or tapestry needle is needed for weaving in loose ends and seaming your finished pieces.

To keep your knitting organized and easily accessible, consider investing in a knitting bag or storage case. These come in various sizes and designs, and often have compartments and pockets to hold your tools and yarn. Having a designated space for your knitting supplies will make it easier to find what you need and keep everything in order.

As you gain more experience and tackle more complex projects, you may find that you need additional tools such as cable needles, stitch counters, or blocking mats.

Creating an Ideal and Comfortable Knitting Space: Creating an ideal and comfortable knitting space is essential for any knitting enthusiast. Having a dedicated area where you can relax, focus, and enjoy your craft can greatly enhance your knitting experience. In this article, we will explore various aspects of creating the perfect knitting space, from choosing the right furniture and lighting to organizing your supplies and adding personal touches.

First and foremost, selecting the right furniture is crucial for creating a comfortable knitting space. A cozy armchair or a comfortable sofa with soft cushions can provide the perfect seating arrangement for long knitting sessions. Consider investing in a chair with good back support to prevent any discomfort or strain on your body. Additionally, having a side table or a small coffee table nearby can be handy for keeping your knitting tools, yarn, and other essentials within reach.

Lighting is another important factor to consider when setting up your knitting space. Natural light is ideal, so try to position your knitting area near a window. This will not only provide ample light but also create a pleasant and inviting atmosphere. However, if natural light is limited, opt for a combination of ambient and task lighting. A floor lamp or a table lamp with adjustable brightness can help you customize the lighting according to your needs.

Organization is key to maintaining a clutter-free and efficient knitting space. Consider investing in storage solutions such as shelves, baskets, or bins to keep your yarn, needles, and other supplies neatly organized. Labeling your storage containers can make it easier to find specific items when you need them.

Additionally, having a designated space for your knitting patterns, books, and magazines can help you stay organized and inspired.

Personal touches can make your knitting space feel truly special and unique. Consider adding decorative elements such as artwork, plants, or a cozy rug to create a warm and inviting ambiance. Displaying finished knitting projects or works in progress can serve as a source of inspiration and motivation. You can also incorporate your favorite colors or patterns into the overall design of the space to reflect your personal style.

Creating a peaceful and serene atmosphere in your knitting space can greatly enhance your knitting experience. Consider adding elements that promote relaxation, such as scented candles, essential oil diffusers, or a small sound system to play soothing music or podcasts. These additions can help create a calming environment and make your knitting sessions even more enjoyable.

In conclusion, creating an ideal and comfortable knitting space involves careful consideration of furniture, lighting, organization, and personal touches.

Finding and Joining the Knitting Community: Finding and joining the knitting community can be a rewarding and fulfilling experience for individuals who are passionate about this craft. Whether you are a beginner or an experienced knitter, being part of a community can provide you with a sense of belonging, opportunities for learning and growth, and a platform to share your creations and ideas.

To start your journey in finding the knitting community, there are several avenues you can explore. One of the most common ways is to join local knitting groups or clubs. These groups often meet regularly, either in person or virtually, to knit together, share patterns, and exchange tips and techniques.

They provide a supportive environment where you can connect with fellow knitters, ask questions, and receive guidance from more experienced members. Local yarn shops are a great resource for finding these groups, as they often host knitting nights or have bulletin boards where you can find information about community events.

In addition to local groups, the internet has opened up a world of possibilities for connecting with the knitting community. Online forums, social media platforms, and knitting websites offer a wealth of resources and opportunities to engage with other knitters from around the world. You can join online knitting communities, participate in virtual knit-alongs, and even take online classes to expand your skills. These platforms also provide a space to showcase your work, seek feedback, and gain inspiration from the diverse range of projects shared by fellow knitters.

Attending knitting retreats, workshops, and conferences is another fantastic way to immerse yourself in the knitting community. These events bring together knitters of all levels and offer a unique opportunity to learn from renowned instructors, discover new techniques, and connect with like-minded individuals who share your passion for knitting. Knitting retreats often take place in picturesque locations, providing a serene and inspiring backdrop for your knitting journey.

Once you have found your place within the knitting community, the benefits are numerous. Being part of a community allows you to tap into a vast pool of knowledge and expertise. You can learn new stitches, explore different knitting styles, and gain insights into the latest trends and patterns. The support and encouragement from fellow knitters can be invaluable, especially during challenging projects or when you encounter difficulties. The knitting community is known for its generosity and willingness to help others, making it a welcoming and inclusive space for all.

Furthermore, being part of a knitting community opens up opportunities for collaboration and creativity. You can participate in group projects, such as charity knitting initiatives or collaborative blankets,…

Techniques and Tips for the Knit Stitch:

The knit stitch is one of the fundamental stitches in knitting, and mastering it is essential for any knitter. Whether you are a beginner or have been knitting for years, there are always techniques and tips that can help improve your knit stitch and make your knitting projects more enjoyable. In this article, we will explore some of these techniques and tips to help you enhance your knitting skills.

1. Proper hand positioning: One of the most important aspects of knitting is having the correct hand positioning. This involves holding the knitting needles in a comfortable and relaxed manner. The right-hand needle should be held like a pencil, while the left-hand needle should be held more loosely. This allows for better control and maneuverability while knitting.

2. Tension control: Maintaining consistent tension is crucial for achieving even and professional-looking stitches. Tension refers to the tightness or looseness of your stitches. If your stitches are too tight, it will be difficult to insert the needle and knit smoothly. On the other hand, if your stitches are too loose, your fabric may appear sloppy and uneven. Practice finding the right balance of tension by experimenting with different hand movements and needle grips.

3. Knitting speed: Knitting speed is a personal preference, but it can greatly affect the outcome of your knit stitches. Some knitters prefer a slower pace to ensure accuracy and control, while others find that a faster speed helps them

maintain a consistent tension. Experiment with different speeds to find what works best for you and your knitting style.

4. Needle size and yarn weight: The size of your knitting needles and the weight of your yarn can also impact your knit stitch. Generally, larger needles are used with thicker yarns, while smaller needles are used with finer yarns. Using the appropriate needle size for your yarn weight will help you achieve the desired fabric density and stitch definition.

5. Practice different knitting styles: There are various knitting styles, such as English knitting, Continental knitting, and Portuguese knitting. Each style has its own unique way of holding the yarn and manipulating the needles. Experimenting with different knitting styles can help you find the one that feels most comfortable and efficient for you.

6. Fixing mistakes: Mistakes happen, even to experienced knitters. Knowing how to fix mistakes in your knit stitch is an essential skill. Whether it's a dropped stitch, a twisted stitch, or a miscounted row, there are techniques to correct these errors without having

Techniques and Tips for the Purl Stitch of Knitting: The purl stitch is one of the fundamental stitches in knitting and is often used in combination with the knit stitch to create various patterns and textures in knitted fabric. While it may seem intimidating at first, with a little practice and some helpful techniques and tips, you'll be purling like a pro in no time.

One of the most important things to remember when working the purl stitch is to hold your yarn correctly. Unlike the knit stitch where the yarn is held in the back of the work, for the purl stitch, you'll need to hold the yarn in the front. This can be done by simply bringing the yarn to the front of your work before inserting the right-hand needle into the stitch.

When inserting the right-hand needle into the stitch, it's important to do so from right to left, going under the left-hand needle. This will ensure that the stitch is properly formed and prevent any twisting or distortion in the fabric. Once the needle is inserted, wrap the yarn around the right-hand needle counterclockwise, making sure to keep the tension consistent.

As you bring the right-hand needle back through the stitch, it's important to maintain an even tension on the yarn. Pulling too tightly can result in a tight and stiff stitch, while not pulling enough can create a loose and sloppy stitch. Finding the right balance may take some practice, but with time, you'll develop a feel for it.

Another helpful tip when purling is to pay attention to your stitch orientation. The purl stitch creates a bump or a "V" shape on the front side of the fabric, while the back side will have a smooth appearance. This can be useful when following a pattern or if you need to identify a specific stitch in your work.

If you find that your purl stitches are too loose or uneven, you can try using a smaller needle size or adjusting your tension. Experimenting with different techniques and finding what works best for you is part of the learning process and can help improve the overall quality of your knitting.

Lastly, practice is key when it comes to mastering the purl stitch. Set aside some dedicated time to practice purling, starting with simple swatches or small projects. As you become more comfortable with the technique, you can challenge yourself with more complex patterns and designs.

Remember, knitting is a skill that takes time and patience to develop. Don't be discouraged if your first attempts at purling aren't perfect.

Combining Knit and Purl Stitches: Ribbing and Textures: When it comes to knitting, there are a variety of stitches that can be combined to create different patterns and textures. One popular technique is combining knit and purl stitches, which allows for the creation of ribbing and various textured designs.

Ribbing is a common knitting technique that is often used for cuffs, collars, and hems. It creates a stretchy and flexible fabric that is perfect for garments that need to fit snugly. Ribbing is achieved by alternating knit and purl stitches in a specific pattern. The most common ribbing pattern is the 1x1 rib, where one knit stitch is followed by one purl stitch, and this pattern is repeated across the row. This creates a series of vertical columns of knit stitches and purl stitches, resulting in a ribbed effect.

Another popular ribbing pattern is the 2x2 rib, where two knit stitches are followed by two purl stitches, and this pattern is repeated across the row. This creates a wider ribbed effect with larger columns of knit and purl stitches. Ribbing can also be done in different combinations, such as 3x1 or 2x1, to create unique and interesting textures.

In addition to ribbing, combining knit and purl stitches can also be used to create various textured designs. By strategically placing knit and purl stitches in different patterns, intricate textures can be achieved. For example, the seed stitch is created by alternating knit and purl stitches in a 1x1 pattern across the row. This creates a bumpy and textured fabric that is visually appealing.

Another textured design that can be created is the moss stitch, which is achieved by alternating knit and purl stitches in a 2x2 pattern across the row. This creates a fabric with small, raised bumps that resemble moss or pebbles. The moss stitch is often used for scarves, blankets, and other cozy accessories.

By combining knit and purl stitches, knitters have the ability to create a wide range of patterns and textures in their projects. Whether it's ribbing for a fitted garment or textured designs for added visual interest, the possibilities are endless. Experimenting with different stitch combinations and patterns can lead to unique and beautiful creations. So, grab your knitting needles and start exploring the world of combining knit and purl stitches to create ribbing and textures in your next project!

Stockinette and Garter Stitch Patterns of Knitting: Stockinette and garter stitch patterns are two of the most basic and commonly used patterns in knitting. These patterns create different textures and appearances in knitted fabric, making them versatile and suitable for a wide range of projects.

The stockinette stitch pattern, also known as the stocking stitch, is created by alternating rows of knit stitches and purl stitches. This pattern produces a smooth and flat fabric with a distinct "V" shape on the right side and a bumpy texture on the wrong side. The stockinette stitch is often used for garments such as sweaters, scarves, and hats, as it creates a sleek and polished look. However, it is important to note that the stockinette stitch tends to curl at the edges, so it is often paired with a border or finished with ribbing to prevent this.

On the other hand, the garter stitch pattern is created by knitting every row, resulting in a fabric with ridges on both sides. This pattern is incredibly simple and is often the first stitch pattern beginners learn. The garter stitch is reversible, meaning it looks the same on both sides, making it ideal for projects where both sides of the fabric will be visible, such as blankets or scarves. Additionally, the garter stitch has a natural tendency to lay flat, making it a great choice for projects that require stability and structure.

Both the stockinette and garter stitch patterns can be used alone or in combination with other stitch patterns to create more intricate designs. For example, a common technique is to use the stockinette stitch for the main body of a garment and the garter stitch for the borders or cuffs. This combination adds visual interest and texture to the finished piece.

It is worth mentioning that the stockinette and garter stitch patterns can be achieved using different knitting techniques, such as hand knitting or machine knitting. Additionally, these patterns can be worked in various yarn weights and fiber types, allowing for endless possibilities in terms of texture and drape.

In conclusion, the stockinette and garter stitch patterns are fundamental in knitting and offer different textures and appearances in the resulting fabric. Whether you are a beginner or an experienced knitter, these patterns can be used to create a wide range of projects, from simple scarves to intricate garments. So grab your knitting needles and yarn, and start exploring the endless possibilities of stockinette and garter stitch knitting!

Seed, Moss, and Other Simple Textured Stitch Patterns of Knitting: Seed, moss, and other simple textured stitch patterns of knitting are versatile and popular choices for adding depth and interest to your knitted projects. These patterns are characterized by their repetitive and easy-to-follow nature, making them suitable for knitters of all skill levels.

The seed stitch, also known as the British moss stitch, is a classic textured pattern that creates a bumpy and reversible fabric. It is achieved by alternating knit and purl stitches within the same row and across subsequent rows. This stitch pattern is perfect for creating a dense and sturdy fabric, making it ideal for scarves, hats, and blankets.

Moss stitch, on the other hand, is similar to the seed stitch but with a slight variation. It is created by working one knit stitch followed by one purl stitch, and then repeating this pattern across the row. In the next row, you simply knit the purl stitches and purl the knit stitches. This creates a fabric with a more pronounced texture and is often used for garments such as sweaters and cardigans.

Apart from the seed and moss stitches, there are numerous other simple textured stitch patterns that can be easily incorporated into your knitting projects. Some examples include the basketweave stitch, which creates a woven-like texture, and the linen stitch, which resembles a woven fabric with its tight and flat appearance.

These textured stitch patterns not only add visual interest to your knitting but also enhance the overall structure and durability of your finished piece. They can be used to create beautiful and unique designs, whether you're knitting a cozy blanket, a stylish scarf, or a trendy sweater.

When working with these stitch patterns, it's important to pay attention to your tension and gauge to ensure an even and consistent fabric. Experimenting with different yarn weights and needle sizes can also yield different results, allowing you to customize the texture and drape of your project.

In conclusion, seed, moss, and other simple textured stitch patterns of knitting offer a wide range of possibilities for adding depth and dimension to your knitted creations. Whether you're a beginner or an experienced knitter, these patterns are a great way to elevate your projects and showcase your skills. So grab your needles, choose your favorite textured stitch pattern, and get ready to create something truly unique and beautiful.

Understanding Cable Construction and Reading Charts of Knitting:

Knitting cables can add a beautiful and intricate design element to your projects. However, understanding cable construction and being able to read charts is essential to successfully incorporate cables into your knitting. In this guide, we will delve into the details of cable construction and provide you with the knowledge and skills to confidently read cable charts.

Cable construction refers to the process of crossing stitches over each other to create a twisted or braided effect. This is achieved by temporarily holding a set of stitches on a cable needle or a spare double-pointed needle, while working the next set of stitches. The held stitches are then worked, either in the same order or in a different order, to create the desired cable pattern. Understanding the basic principles of cable construction will enable you to create a wide variety of cable designs.

Reading cable charts is an important skill to master when working with cables. Cable charts are visual representations of the cable patterns, typically presented in a grid format. Each square on the chart represents a stitch, and the symbols or colors within the square indicate the type of stitch to be worked. By following the chart row by row, you can easily keep track of the cable pattern and ensure that your cables are worked correctly.

To read a cable chart, start by identifying the key or legend that explains the symbols used in the chart. This will help you understand the different types of stitches and their corresponding symbols. Once you are familiar with the symbols, begin reading the chart from right to left for right-side rows and from left to right for wrong-side rows. Each row of the chart represents a specific row of knitting, so it is important to follow the chart in the correct order.

When working with cable charts, it is also important to pay attention to the stitch count. Cable patterns often require a specific number of stitches to be worked in order to create the desired cable effect. Make sure to count your stitches before and after each cable section to ensure that you have the correct number of stitches. If you find that you have too many or too few stitches, you may need to adjust your knitting or consult the pattern for guidance.

In addition to understanding cable construction and reading charts, it is helpful to have a few tips and tricks up your sleeve when working with cables. One common technique is to use a cable needle or a spare double-pointed needle to hold the stitches while crossing them. This prevents the stitches from unraveling and ensures that the cable is worked correctly

INTRODUCTION

Once you've mastered knitting and purling, you can tackle nearly any knitting pattern, if you've got the concentration and focus. Even the most complex knitting patterns are made up of knit stitches, purl stitches, increases and decreases. These same stitches produce cables, lace, and brioche stitch. They are used for mosaic, stranded, intarsia and double knitting.

This book is a stitch dictionary, providing you with the ability to look up a wide variety of knitting patterns. The first chapters provide you with an introduction or review of knitting and purling, followed by a detailed look at different types of increases and decreases. Next, you'll find a chapter devoted to knitting gauge with a simple formula for an afghan square, dishcloth or simple scarf. This formula will allow you to use any of the stitch patterns to create a practice piece that you can use and enjoy.

Knitting patterns can be in written form or charted, so we'll review how to read a knitting pattern, including common abbreviations and chart symbols. While they're not always standardized, a style sheet will help you decipher most knitting patterns, and will show you how to read the charts in this book. Here, we'll also introduce some helpful tools for pattern knitting to help you keep track of your place, reduce errors and stitch your way to success. You'll find the patterns in this book in both written, and where helpful, charted form.

The first pattern chapters review simple pattern stitches, including various types of ribbing, seed and moss stitch. Later chapters introduce cables, lace and other knitting techniques, building upon what you already know. Knit swatches or project examples illustrate stitches of various sorts, along with pattern charts, and where necessary diagrams. When special tools or techniques are required, we'll share those too for each type of stitch pattern.

These stitch patterns don't tell you how to knit a sweater or a pair of socks; however, experienced knitters can work out their gauge and integrate a stitch pattern into another pattern. For example adding a lace panel to the front of a sweater or working cables into their sock pattern. Beginners or intermediate knitters will find these stitch patterns an ideal way to practice skills, whether you opt for a simple square washcloth or knit an entire scarf. You can even combine patterns and knit a sample scarf or afghan to master a wide variety of stitch patterns in a single project.

CHAPTER 1: KNITTING AND PURLING

If you're using this book, you likely already know how to knit and purl. However, if you're returning to knitting after a long absence, a review won't hurt. We've also included a quick guide to some common errors that may not be noticeable on simple knitting, but can rapidly become apparent as you move into more complex knitting patterns. Since this is a stitch dictionary, rather than a how-to-knit book, we're not covering casting on or binding off in this book. You'll also want to check your favorite beginner knitting book or website for an overview of English and Continental knitting styles, as well as hybrids of the two. You can knit any pattern using the method you prefer—as long as it produces even stitches that face the right way, you're good to go.

The knit stitch and the purl stitch are the basic building blocks of all knitting patterns. Worked flat with each row knit, the knit stitch produces garter stitch. Worked in the round or in tandem with purl rows, the knit stitch produces stockinette stitch. Knit and purl stitches combine on the right side of the work to form ribbing, seed and moss stitch patterns. These stitches are also an essential part of nearly every other knitting pattern. They're also the basis of increase and decrease stitches of all sorts.

Knit stitches always begin with the yarn behind the work and your work facing you. To make a knit stitch, insert the tip of the right hand needle into the front loop of the first stitch on the left hand needle. The needle is inserted from below the stitch, moving upward and toward the back. It should, when properly placed, be sitting directly behind the left hand needle before you progress with the stitch. Pull up a loop, either by picking, in the Continental style, or throwing, in the English style. You now have both the original stitch on the left hand needle and the newly created stitch on the right hand needle. Drop the original stitch off of the left hand needle. You've now completed one knit stitch. Knit stitches look like v's when viewed from the front side of the work.

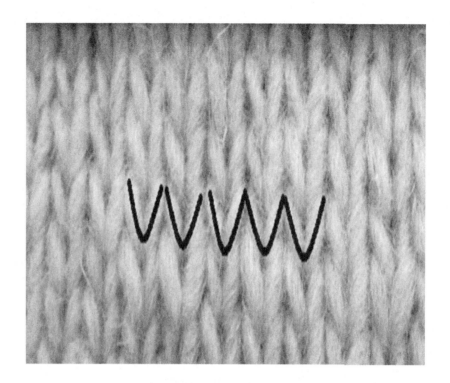

The purl stitch is essentially the reverse of the knit stitch. When purling, the yarn should be to the front of the work, facing you. To purl, you will insert the right hand needle into the front loop of the first stitch on the left hand needle. Rather than inserting the needle up and back, it will go down and forward. Pick or wrap the yarn around the needle in a downward, counter-clockwise direction and pull the new purl stitch through the loop. Drop the old stitch off of the left and needle. Purl stitches look like horizontal bumps when viewed from the front of the work. The backside of a knit stitch is a purl stitch and the backside of a purl stitch is a knit stitch.

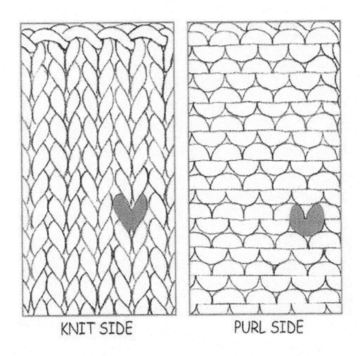

KNIT SIDE   PURL SIDE

Occasionally, and even in this book, you'll see a pattern ask you to knit or purl through the back loop. While both knit and purl stitches are normally worked through the front loop of the stitch, occasionally the stitch is twisted. Twisted stitches are typically created by knitting through the back loop, rather than the front loop, of the stitch. The twisted stitch has a slightly different appearance than one knitted through the front loop.

COMMON PROBLEMS

There are a few relatively common problems with the basic knit and purl stitch. First, some people will begin knitting through the back loop, twisting every stitch. While this happens occasionally, it is much more common for new knitters or even intermediate knitters to twist purl stitches. A twisted stitch will present on the needle the wrong way, with the back loop closer to the end of the needle than the front loop. Purl stitches are not typically twisted by purling through the back loop, but by wrapping the yarn in the wrong, or a clockwise direction. If you find twisted stitches in your work, you can correct the alignment of the stitch on the needle by knitting through the back loop of the twisted stitch.

Other common problems with basic knit and purl stitches include dropped stitches, skipped stitches, accidental yarn overs, or knitting with the wrong end of the yarn. Follow this quick section to correct these mistakes in your knitting. Many of these fix-it tips will work for more complex knitting patterns as well as simple ones.

Dropped Stitch

A dropped stitch is just what it sounds like. A stitch has been dropped from the needles. This may happen as you knit or if a needle has pulled out of your work at some point. It may be easily accessible or may have dropped several rows, leaving you with a visible row of ladders in your knitting, or horizontal bars, a lot like the run in a pair of pantyhose. You'll need a crochet hook and good lighting to fix this error. Locate the dropped stitch and pick it up with the crochet hook. Review the pattern to determine how many rows you have to bring the stitch up and which rows are knitted and which are purled stitches. With the crochet hook, pull the horizontal ladder of yarn through the picked up stitch to create a knit stitch. If you need to create a purl stitch, bring the ladder forward in front of the picked up stitch and pull it back and through the stitch. Continue pulling up stitches until you've brought the dropped stitch in line with your work. Replace the stitch on the left hand needle and knit normally according to your pattern.

Missed Yarn-Over

Correcting a missed yarn over can be somewhat more difficult, depending upon your personal tension. If you're knitting relatively loosely and have missed a yarn over, you may be able to drop down a row or two and catch the ladder between stitches to create the yarn over and knit it according to the pattern. If you've added a yarn over and you're knitting loosely, simply removing it will leave you with an unsightly loose area in your knitting. Unfortunately, the best solution in that case is to rip back or "frog" your knitting and reknit. If you're a very tight knitter and it's a relatively forgiving yarn, you may be able to drop the unwanted yarn over and take up the slack in the surrounding stitches without dramatically impacting your work. You can also, in some cases, take in the extra yarn over with a decrease. In some patterns, this may not show at all; however, in others it can be quite obvious. Use your own discretion when you decide whether you want to try to fix an "oops" or simply redo the work to re-knit it correctly.

Skipped or Slipped Stitch

If you've skipped or accidentally slipped a stitch in your knitting, you should be able to see a ladder, or horizontal length of yarn on the wrong side of that row. Just as you fixed a dropped stitch, you can drop back and fix a skipped stitch in the same way. If you catch it on the next row, there's no need for a crochet hook and it's easy to knit the missed stitch using the ladder of yarn. Depending upon the pattern, a missed stitch or slipped stitch may be hard to see. If you can't find it, neither can anyone else. This is one mistake that can normally be left in your work without causing serious problems.

Now that we've covered the basics, let's move on to what you need to know to make this book work for you.

CHAPTER 2: SWATCHES AND SQUARES

Nearly every knitter has experienced the horror of realizing that a project is too-small or too-large. While knitting patterns include a recommended needle size, gauge, or the number of stitches and rows you get to the inch, can vary dramatically. One person may be a very tight knitter and another, an extremely loose knitter. For these two to produce the same size garment using the same pattern and yarn, they need to use very different size needles. How do you know what size needle to use, what size garment to make and how to produce something that fits? Will you even like how the given yarn looks in this stitch pattern or knit to this gauge?

Fortunately, there's a simple, if sometimes time-consuming, solution to all of these questions. Knit a gauge swatch. A gauge swatch is typically a square of knitting, often around 6-inches by 6-inches. For knitting in the round, the most accurate result comes from a swatch knit in the round. You should knit your swatch in pattern. For example, if you're working on a lace sock, the gauge in the lace pattern matters. In a worsted weight yarn, plan on a 36-stitch to 40-stitch wide gauge swatch for the greatest accuracy. Knit the first three or four stitches of each row front and back to create a garter stitch edging for a flatter and easier to measure swatch. For some yarns, you may need to wash and block your swatch for the most accurate gauge. There is one cheat possible here; if you're willing to knit a bit further, on some patterns you can opt to start by knitting a sleeve, pocket or other small section.

To measure the gauge on your swatch, lay it out flat. You may, depending upon the yarn, find it helpful to pin it in place with sewing pins. Use a ruler or a knitting gauge to measure a 4-inch square. Count the number of stitches and the number of rows. Typically, gauge is calculated over a 4-inch swatch, for instance, 18 stitches to 4 inches. Occasionally, particularly for bulky yarns, you'll find the stitch count recorded per inch, for instance 3 ½ stitches per inch. Count the rows vertically to determine row count, typically recorded as 20 rows to 4 inches. Note down your gauge and needle size. Compare these to the recommended gauge for the pattern. If you have too many stitches to the inch, go up a needle size and knit another gauge swatch. If you have too few stitches, go down a needle size to achieve the correct gauge. Sometimes, you may get stitch gauge with your yarn, but not row gauge.

While row gauge matters, depending upon the pattern, you may find it easy to correct for row gauge issues. For instance, if your pattern asks you to knit to 16-inches, the row gauge doesn't matter much at all. If, on the other hand, you're told to knit 72 rows, you'll need to recalculate to determine the correct length. This is a simple matter of math if you know the desired row gauge and your row gauge. For example, if 24 rows equal 4-inches on the pattern, 72 rows will equal 12-inches. If you're getting 22 rows per 4-inches, you'll need to knit 66 rows to reach the 12-inch length needed. You can make similar adjustments for stitch gauge; however, they're significantly more complex. You're typically better off choosing a needle size or yarn that better matches the pattern gauge.

Gauge swatches also provide you with information about the drape, texture and density of your fabric. You may, for instance, find that you don't like the way a certain yarn knits at a given gauge. You can, by increasing needle size, knit a yarn at a looser gauge for a more open fabric, or opt for a smaller needle and a tighter gauge for a very dense fabric. Lace projects, typically worked in fingering or lace weight yarn, routinely use a needle much larger than that suggested for the yarn. A project that needs to be durable, such as a potholder, may be knit more tightly than normal.

Simple Project For Your Extra Swatches

Now that you know why you need to check your gauge, what on earth do you do with all of those gauge swatches? Well, for some yarns, including cotton, bamboo, linen and hemp, your gauge swatch can make a lovely and usable washcloth, facecloth or dishcloth as-is. Swatches of worsted weight wool can be sewn together to form an afghan or hand-knit quilt. If you plan to use them as a quilt, work all squares with a 4 row/4 stitch garter border. This pattern is designed for a gauge of 20 stitches/24 rows to 4-inches. Adjust it if your gauge varies.

-Cast on 40 stitches. Knit 4 rows.

-Row 1: K4, knit 32 stitches in pattern, K4

-Row 2: K4, purl 32 stitches in pattern, K4

-Repeat row 1 and 2 until you have completed 16 repeats, or 36 total rows, counting the first 4 knit rows.

-Knit 4 rows. Bind off.

If your stitch pattern doesn't work in a multiple of 2, 4, 8 or 16, you can easily begin your pattern after a two to three stitch garter edge or extend the garter edging if needed.

Alternatives To Knitting Swatches

You can also opt for a small project instead of a swatch to determine whether you like a stitch pattern with a given yarn and needle size. If you're working with a pattern that is largely garter or ribbing, like seed stitch that will lie flat without curling, there's no need for a garter or seed stitch edge. For stockinette stitch and similar patterns, including most lace and cabling, you will want a garter or seed stitch edge to stabilize your knitting. We've provided two simple schemes, one to make a scarf and the other a cowl.

-Step 1: Guess your gauge. This project is taking the place of a swatch, so there's no swatching here. If you know you're a tight knitter or a loose knitter, adjust accordingly, but you can often estimate gauge based on the yarn label.

-Step 2: Do the math. First, check the pattern you like. If it's an 8-stitch repeat, you need your body stitches in a multiple of 8. You also want your scarf to be an appropriate width, typically 6 to 10 inches. If you're working with a yarn that you expect to get 5-stitches to the inch and you want an 8-inch wide scarf, you need 40 stitches total. You'll have 4 border stitches on each side, plus three repeats of your 8-stitch pattern. Cast on 40 stitches.

-Step 3: Work 4 rows of garter stitch before you begin knitting in pattern, unless, as noted above, you've chosen a pattern that will lie flat. Start knitting in pattern, maintaining a 4-stitch border on each side. Work to the desired length and finish with 4 rows of garter stitch. Bind off.

If you'd prefer to make a cowl or infinity scarf, the general process is similar. Measure your favorite cowl to determine the approximate measurements. Let's say you want a cowl 30-inches around and 8-inches deep. You'll need to cast on around 150 stitches, depending upon your stitch pattern. Since the cowl will be worked in the round, you don't need edging stitches, but you do need your math to work. If your stitch pattern has 12 stitches, you should cast on a multiple of 12, like 144.

-Step 1: Do the math. Determine your desired length, approximate gauge and planned stitch pattern. Cast on the correct number of stitches.

-Step 2: Work 3 to 4 rows of k1, p1 ribbing or garter stitch.

-Step 3: Begin working in pattern until approximately 3/4-inch from desired width. Work 3 to 4 rows of ribbing or garter stitch to complete your cowl.

Other possibilities for small projects you can do include pillow fronts, bag inserts, or potholders. While you may want to use your gauge swatches, if you're short on yarn, you can also rip out your gauge swatch and make it part of the project. Some knitters even save and organize their swatches, marking them with the type of needle, size of needle, yarn information and more. While these are a valuable reference, they can also provide you with yarn if you should need to mend your knitting in the future.

CHAPTER 3: READING YOUR PATTERNS

There's no universal style guide for knitting patterns. Chart keys and even written abbreviations can vary; however, here's an easy introduction that helps you decipher most of the common symbols and abbreviations.

-k: Knit:

-p: Purl

-K2tog: knit two together

-P2tog: purl two together

-SSK: slip, slip, knit

-SSP: slip, slip, purl

-Sl: slip

-Sl1, k1, psso: slip one, knit one, pass the slipped stitch over

-Sl1, k2tog, psso: slip one, knit two together, pass the slipped stitch over

-YO: yarn over

-KFB: knit front and back

-PFB: purl front and back

-M1L: make one left

-M1R: make one right

These abbreviations are used in most knitting patterns. For instance, ribbing might be written as k2,p2 to end of row. You'll also see parentheses used, like k4 (yo, k2tog) repeat from () until 4 stitches remain. While simple patterns are typically written out like this, lace and cables, as well as colorwork use charts in place of words or along with words.

Below, is an example of a simple lace knitting chart. You will notice that only the right-side rows are charted on the lace chart. In some cases, you'll see the wrong-side rows charted. You'll read this chart from right-to-left. If your chart includes both right and wrong side rows, the even numbered rows are read left-to-right. Row numbers tell you what to knit when. While this sample chart is numbered 1, 3 and 5, in many projects, the row numbers will be higher, since you'll be adding lace panels to an already started knitting project.

Written out, this pattern reads:

-Row 1: k3, (k2, yo, k2tog, ssk, yo, k2) to last 3 stitches. K3.

-Row 2: K3, purl to end, K3

-Row 3: K3, (k1, yo, k2tog, k2, ssk, yo, k1) to last 3 stitches, k3.

-Row 4: Repeat row 2

-Row 5: K3, (yo, k2tog, k4, ssk, yo) to last 3 stitches, k3.

Legend

☐ k (knit)

O yo (yarnover)

\ ssk (slip, slip knit)

/ k2tog (knit two together)

Just like a map, the legend or key below the chart tells you what each symbol means. While more complex symbols may vary, some basic ones are pretty common. Blank squares are typically knit stitches on right-side rows and purl stitches on wrong-side rows. A straight horizontal line typically represents purl stitches on the right side or knit stitches on the wrong side; however, occasionally k and p will take the place of these. Angled lines like / and \ commonly represent basic decreases. If you look at the line, you can "read" the decrease. The first of these / represents k2tog while \ represents ssk. An empty circle is a fairly standard symbol for a yarn over. Just knowing and recognizing these symbols will help you get started with new knitting stitches and patterns.

Charts are also typically used for cable knitting. These charts are similar to the ones used for lace knitting. Right-side rows are read right-to-left and wrong-side rows left to right. Remember, if you're knitting in the round, they're all right side rows. Cable charts may include typical symbols, like those for knit, purl, increases and decreases, but also have charted cables. The symbols for cables on a chart may be as small as 2-stitches wide or, for a very large cable, can take up many more stitches. Your symbol indicates whether you're cabling toward the front or back, whether you're knitting or purling, and which stitches are to be knitted and which should be purled. See the chart below for a sample of what to expect when you look at cable knitting charts.

Written out, this cable pattern looks like this:

-P2, K2, P2, K2, P4, K2, P2, K2, P2

-K2, P2, K2, P2, K4, P2, K2, P2, K2

-P2, K2, P2, K2, P4, K2, P2, K2, P2

-K2, P2, K2, P2, CL2 or CF2, P2, K2, P2, K2

-P2, K2, P2, K2, P4, K2, P2, K2, P2

-K2, P2, K2, P2, K4, P2, K2, P2, K2

The cable, represented by the partially colored in symbols creating an X, may be referred to as CL, cable left, or CF, cable front. In this case, the first two stitches are held to the front of the work, the next two worked, then the first two stitches are worked creating a simple cable. It crosses in the front and to the left, hence the reference to CL or CF. The X-shape or shading is typically reversed for a cable crossing in the back. You'll also see purl stitch symbols in some cable symbols, indicating that a portion of the stitches are to be purled rather than knit.

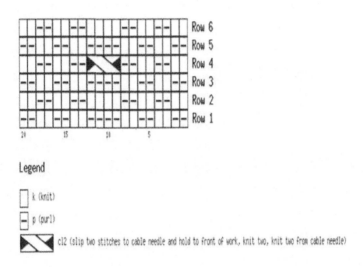

Legend

☐ k (knit)

⊟ p (purl)

◪ cl2 (slip two stitches to cable needle and hold to front of work, knit two, knit two from cable needle)

For the stitch patterns, in this book, each chart will be accompanied by a key, but the symbols will be standardized. When you're knitting from commercial patterns from a book, magazine, website or independent designer, check their key or legend to determine what's what on the chart. You will soon begin to recognizing common symbols and be able to read charts without too much difficulty.

The other thing you need to understand is how charts repeat. You'll need to know this whether you're knitting a commercial pattern or creating your own with one of the stitch patterns in this dictionary. Frequently, charts will have two heavy lines marking a single repeat of the chart, with slightly different stitch patterns before and after the repeat. In this case, you'll start the row from the right hand edge; however, you won't work all the way to the left hand edge. You'll work up to the second solid black line or shaded area, then restart from the beginning of the repeat. If you're adding one of the stitch patterns included in this book to a pattern you've purchased or designed, you'll want to graph it out in a similar way. This allows you to maintain the integrity of the lace or cables, while adjusting for increases or decreases as needed.

Most knitting charts tell you what stitch to use at a given point in a pattern. Colorwork charts are similar, but they provide information about what color to use. Some charts, particularly if you're increasing or decreasing, may include a few symbols. Unlike most charts, colorwork charts are typically printed in color, with different color squares indicating different yarns. If your pattern includes white, light blue, bright blue and navy, you'll see three distinguishable shades of blue, plus uncolored squares on your chart. Older colorwork charts may not be in color. In this case, they'll rely on symbols to indicate each color. If you're familiar with cross stitch charts, the appearance is similar. One color might be marked by a dot, another by a slash and a third by an open circle. You can make these charts easier to follow by coloring the chart with colored pencils before you start. Coloring the chart makes it readable at a glance.

Charts can be confusing the first time or two you use one. Before you tackle your first big lace or cable project, try mastering the chart by using a simple charted stitch pattern to make a scarf or other item, as laid out in the previous chapter. Now, let's cover some tips and tricks for tackling more complex knitting patterns.

CHAPTER 4: TIPS, TRICKS AND TOOLS

The key to working with more complex stitch patterns, like the ones included in this book, is to keep track of where you are in your knitting. If you lose your place, whether it's not knowing which row you're on or which stitch you're on, you may find yourself ripping and ripping. Keeping track of where you are, finding your place if you're lost and salvaging nearly hopeless knitting are all essential tricks.

Tracking Rows

Everyone has their own method of tracking rows in a chart. Some knitters find they do fine keeping track in their head, particularly if a pattern has a relatively short (less than 10 row) repeat and is easy to track by sight. While it's a bit low-tech, a printed copy of your pattern (it's legal to make a working copy of magazines and books you own) and a highlighter or highlighter tape is an easy option to track your progress. The highlighter works well if you are only working a chart once, but if you're knitting the same chart repeatedly, you may want highlighter tape. Magnetic chart holders allow you to track your progress by moving a magnetic bar. With a magnetic bar chart holder, you can move the bar up and down as needed to track your progress.

Row Counters

If you don't carry a paper copy or you don't want to mark up a paper copy, row counters can help. Choose from the traditional row counter, a modern alternative or even a smartphone or tablet app. Traditional row counters act like a stitch marker on your knitting. You'll click the marker as you finish each row or round, adding a row to your count. Smartphone and tablet apps work in the same way, but with a tap at the end of each round or row. Less common are beaded counters. You'll track rows by moving beads from place to place. Typically, a second strand of beads denotes every 10 rows.

Stitch Markers

Stitch markers are the best way to track your stitches, make sure your stitch count is correct, and avoid missed or extra stitches. You'll nearly always see a stitch marker recommended to mark the beginning of the round if you're working on circular or double point needles, but they can do much more than that. You can use stitch markers to track elements in a pattern, like increases or decreases, if you're knitting a garment or similar item. If you're working in a repeating pattern, like lace, cables or some types of colorwork, you can place a marker between each repeat. This is an easy way to track your accuracy. If you have 12 stitches per repeat and you suddenly reach the end of a 12-stitch repeat with two stitches left, you can spot your error quickly and easily. For larger projects, stitch markers can also help you to track your stitch count, whether you're casting on, increasing or decreasing.

Stitch markers are available in a variety of forms, from simple rings to detachable markers that look a bit like a safety pin. The inexpensive ring style markers are popular, effective and are not particularly cumbersome. Your knitting won't catch on these simple markers. Handmade markers with beads or other ornaments are a fun accent to your knitting; however, if you're working with lace or another delicate project, these may catch in your knitting. Detachable markers work very well if you expect to need to move your markers from place to place, rather than row to row. Keep in mind that you may want to have markers of different colors, especially for lace knitting. There are a number of cheap and practical DIY marker options, including tiny silicone hair bands, small lengths of drinking straws, or simple yarn loops. You can even use small O-rings from your local hardware store.

Lifelines

There's one more tip or trick that's essential if you're working with heavily patterned knitting—the lifeline. A lifeline is a length of sturdy, relatively stiff thread, like crochet cotton or even dental floss. You'll hold it against your needle as you knit or thread it through the stitches on your needle once they're knit. If you do find an unfixable error, the lifeline will secure this row of stitches, allowing you to rip back a few rows or a single repeat, rather than potentially losing all of your hard work. You can opt to run a lifeline every 10 rows, every 20, or every repeat, depending upon your comfort level.

Some of these tools aren't essential and others are must-haves, but as you can see, you can make do with makeshift tools, free smartphone apps or even a sheet of paper and a row of check marks. Either way, learning to track and mark your progress will help you keep your place during even the most complex knitting projects.

CHAPTER 5: SIMPLE STITCH PATTERNS

STOCKINETTE

Written out for flat knitting:

-Knit one row, purl one row

-You'll always knit on the right side and purl on the wrong side.

Worked in the round:

-Knit all stitches

-This is true whether you're using circular or double-point needles

REVERSE STOCKINETTE

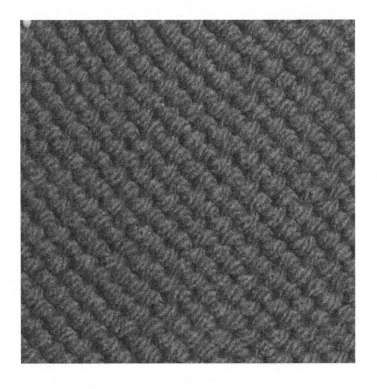

Written out for flat knitting:

-Purl one row, knit one row

-You'll purl on the right side and knit on the wrong side.

Worked in the round:

-Purl all rows

TEXTURED STRIPES

Textured stripes alternate stockinette and reverse stockinette. While you can make the stripes any width you choose, the following will provide you with an idea of how to work these stripes.

Worked flat or in the round:

Use the standard directions for each stitch pattern:

-Work 4 rows stockinette, work 4 rows reverse stockinette.

-Repeat to desired length. You can work textured stripes in a single color or multiple colors.

GARTER

Written out for flat knitting:

-Knit all rows

Worked in the round:

-Knit one row, purl one row

RIBBING

Ribbing is a pattern of knit and purl stitches that forms vertical ribs or lines in your knitting. This is highly elastic and practical for brims, cuffs and edgings. You can adjust ribbing to the width you desire, from a 1x1 ribbing to a much larger one.

Written out for flat knitting:

-Knit two stitches, purl two stitches, repeat to the end

-On the reverse, you'll purl two stitches, then knit two stitches

-Work in a multiple of four for 2x2 ribbing

Worked in the round:

-Knit two stitches, purl two stitches to the end of round

RIBBING THROUGH THE BACK LOOP

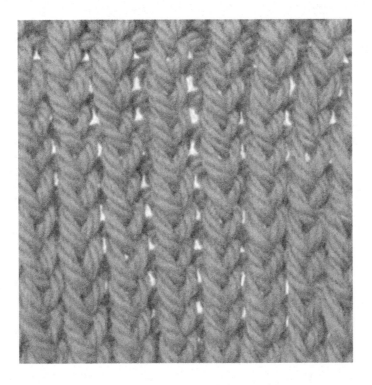

Working through the back loop creates a twist in your knit stitches.

Written out for flat knitting:

-Knit two stitches through the back loop, purl two stitches, repeat to the end

-On the reverse, you'll purl two stitches through the back loop, then knit two stitches

-Again, you'll work in a multiple of 4 for 2x2 ribbing

Worked in the round:

-Knit two stitches through the back loop, purl two stitches on all rounds

GARTER RIBBING

Garter ribbing is relatively uncommon, but it is quite simple.

Written out for flat knitting:

-Knit two stitches, purl two stitches, knit two stitches, repeat to the end of row

-Repeat on the reverse to create garter stitch

Worked in the round:

-Knit two stitches, purl two stitches, knit two stitches, repeat to the end of row

-On the next row, purl two stitches, knit two stitches, purl two stitches to the end of row

RICE STITCH

Rice stitch is a textured stitch that works especially well for dishcloths and similar items.

Written out for flat knitting:

-Purl one, knit one through the back loop, purl one to the end of the row, knit across on the reverse

-Work in a multiple of 2 + 1, ie. 25 stitches

Worked in the round:

-Purl one, knit one through the back loop, purl one to the end of the row, purl across on the reverse

SEED STITCH

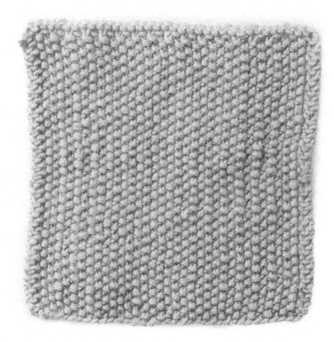

Seed stitch lays flat, adds textural interest and is a popular alternative to ribbing or garter stitch. Works in any multiple.

Worked flat or in the round:

-Knit one, purl one to the end of row

-On the reverse, purl one, knit one

DOUBLE SEED STITCH

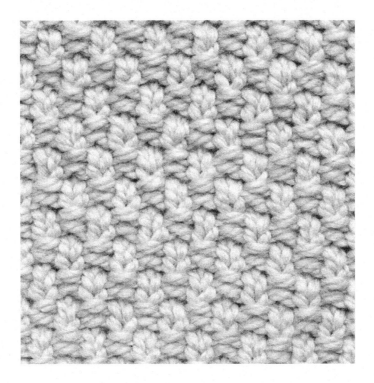

Double seed stitch is a simple variation on seed stitch. Like seed stitch, it is worked the same flat or in the round.

Worked flat or in the round:

-Row 1: Knit one, purl one to the end of row

-Row 2: Knit one, purl one to the end of row

-Row 3: Purl one, knit one to the end of row

-Row 4: Purl one, knit one to the end of row

-Repeat as many times as needed

BASKETWEAVE

Basketweave stitch produces a defined stitch alternating panels of stockinette and reverse stockinette. This is a 12-row repeat, worked in a multiple of 8.

Written out for flat knitting:

-Row 1: Knit

-Row 2, 4, 6: Knit 4, purl 4 to end of the row

-Row 3, 5: Purl 4, knit 4 to end of the row

-Row 7: Knit

-Row 8, 10, 12: Purl 4, knit 4 to end of the row

-Row 9, 11: Knit 4, purl 4 to end of the row

Worked in the round:

-Row 1: Knit

-Row 2-6: Knit 4, purl 4 to the end of row

-Row 7: Knit

-Row 8-12: Purl 4, knit 4 to the end of row

CHAPTER 6: SLIP STITCHES

SIMPLE SLIP STITCH

A simple slip stitch pattern can create vertical stripes without carrying your yarn or weaving in ends. This makes slip stitch patterns a practical and easy alternative for a variety of projects, whether you use them as a stripe or an accent in two or three colors. The pattern below is simply a guideline. Directions are provided for knitting flat, but the same concept is easy to adapt to knitting in the round. You'll slip the yarn with the yarn in front or yarn in back and typically, have pattern notes telling you whether to slip purlwise or knitwise.

This is a brick stitch pattern, but the same idea can be used for a variety of other slip stitch knitting patterns. Knit in a multiple of 4 + 3, i.e. 27.

Written out for flat knitting:

-Rows 1 and 2: Knit in color 1

-Row 3: Using color 2, knit 1, *slip 1 with yarn in back, knit 3. Repeat from * to last 2 stitches, slip 1, knit 1

-Row 4: With color 2, purl 1, *slip 1 with yarn in front, purl 3. Repeat from * to last 2 stitches, slip 1, purl 1

-Rows 5 and 6: With color 1, knit

-Row 7: With color 2, *knit 3, slip 1 with yarn in back. Repeat from * across

-Row 8: With color 2, *purl 3, slip 1 with yarn in front. Repeat from * across

-Repeat these 8 rows for pattern

MOSAIC KNITTING

Mosaic knitting relies upon slipped stitches to create patterned knitting. Mosaic knitting looks quite complex, but is really quite simple. As is true for other slipped stitch patterns, you will need to begin your work with rows of color two. As for other slip stitch patterns, this is written for flat knitting but can be altered to accommodate knitting in the round. You'll find that mosaic knitting can often mimic the appearance of fair isle or other types of colorwork.

-Row 1-2: Knit in color 1

-Row 2-3: Knit in color 2

-Begin knitting from the chart. Read right-side rows right to left and left side rows left to right. Knit all uncolored stitches on the right side and purl on the wrong side. Slip all colored stitches purlwise. Mosaic knitting is always worked from a chart, typically one that looks much like the following picture.

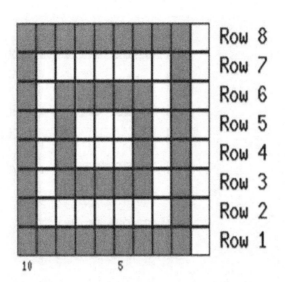

Row 8
Row 7
Row 6
Row 5
Row 4
Row 3
Row 2
Row 1

DIAGONAL SLIP STITCH

The diagonal slip stitch pattern produces clean, diagonal lines across a background of stockinette stitch. This is an 8 row repeat, worked in a multiple of 4 + 2.

-Row 1: k1, *k3, p1, repeat from * to 1 stitch from end, k1

-Row 2: k1, *slip 1 wyib, p3, repeat from * to 1 stitch from end, k1

-Row 3: k1, *k3, slip 1 wyif, repeat from * to 1 stitch from end, k1

-Row 4: k1, *drop slipped stitch and move to the front of the work, p2, knit the dropped stitch, p1, repeat from * to 1 stitch from end, k1

-Row 5: k2, *p1, k3, repeat from * to end

-Row 6: k1, *p2, slip 1 wyib, p1, repeat from * to end

-Row 7: k2, *slip 1 wyif, k3, repeat from * to end

-Row 8: k1, *p2, drop slipped stitch and move to the front of the work, p2, knit the dropped stitch, repeat from * to last three stitches, drop the slipped stitch to the front of work, p1, purl the dropped stitch, k1

SLIP STITCH HONEYCOMB

Unlike the previous slip stitch patterns, directions are provided both in the round and flat for this one.

Written out for flat knitting:

-Row 1: Knit

-Row 2: Knit 1, slip 1 wyif, repeat to end of row

-Row 3: Knit

-Row 4: Slip 1 wyif, knit 1, repeat to end of row

Worked in the round:

-Round 1: Knit

-Round 2: *Purl 1, slip 1 wyif* repeat across round.

-Round 3: Knit

-Round 4 : *Slip 1 wyif, Purl 1* repeat across round.

SMOCKING STITCH

Written out for flat knitting:

Written for flat knitting, this pattern creates an appearance similar to hand-sewn smocking, with stitches gathering to form a diamond pattern.

-Row 1 (Wrong Side): P3, *k2, p4,* repeat from * to last 3 sts, p3

-Row 2: K3, *sl 2, k4,* repeat from * to last 3 sts, k3

-Row 3: P3, *sl 2, p4,* repeat from * to last 3 sts, p3

-Row 4: K1, *sl next 2 sts on spare needle and leave at back, k1, k 2 off the spare needle, sl next stitch on spare needle, and leave at front, k2, k1 off spare needle,* repeat from * to last stitch, k1

-Row 5: P6, *k2, p4,* repeat from * to last 6 sts, p6

-Row 6: K6, *sl 2, k4,* repeat from * to last 6 sts, k6

-Row 7: P6, *sl 2, p4,* repeat from * to last 6 sts, p6

-Row 8: K4, *sl next 2 sts on spare needle and leave at back, k1, k 2 off spare needle, sl next stitch on spare needle and leave at front, k2, k 1 off spare needle,* repeat from * to last 4 sts, k4

CHAPTER 7: CABLES

RIGHT CABLES

A right cable crosses to the right. Stitches are moved from the left, and over toward the right to create the right cable. The stitches from the right are held to the back during the cable cross. You'll see the same cable called either a "cr" for cable right or a "cb" for cable back. It's the exact same stitch and is charted in the same way. If you're working from the written instructions, the number usually announces how many stitches you're moving, so a cr2 involves four stitches in total.

Make a cable right or cable back by moving stitches to a cable needle. Hold the cable needle to the back and knit the next stitches in the cable from the left hand needle. Knit the stitches off the cable needle. You've now completed a cable right. The same cable can be done with as few as two stitches or as many as 16. The cable symbol will note how many stitches are included in the cable. The cable may also be done with a combination of knit and purl stitches, but the symbol is slightly different. In most cases, a short straight line marks purl stitches in the cable.

Cables are typically charted, like this:

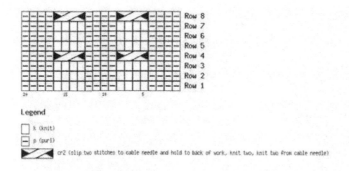

Legend

☐ k (knit)

⊟ p (purl)

◤◥ cr2 (slip two stitches to cable needle and hold to back of work, knit two, knit two from cable needle)

Written out for flat knitting:

-Rows 1-3: Purl 4, knit 4, purl 4, knit 4, purl 4

-Row 4: Purl 4, cr2, purl 4, cr2, purl 4

-Row 5-7: Purl 4, knit 4, purl 4, knit 4, purl 4

-Row 8: Purl 4, cr2, purl 4, cr2, purl 4

LEFT CABLES

A left cable crosses to the left. Stitches are held to the front to create a left-leaning cable. This cable may be called a "cl" for cable left or a "cf" for cable front. The cable left is typically noted with the number of stitches moved, so a cl2 moves two stitches and is worked over four stitches in total.

Make a cable left or cable front by moving stitches to a cable needle. Hold the cable needle to the front and knit the next stitches in the cable from the left hand needle. Knit the stitches off the cable needle. You've now completed a cable left. The same cable can be done with as few as two stitches or as many as 16. Larger cables are marked with a larger symbol on the chart. The cable symbol will always cover as many stitches as are included in the cable. The cable may also be done with a combination of knit and purl stitches, but the symbol is slightly different. In most cases, a short straight line marks purl stitches in the cable.

The left cable is charted like this:

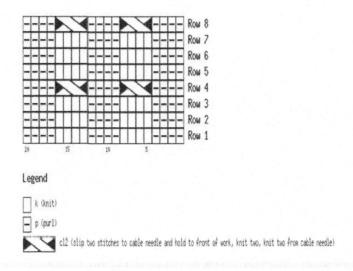

Written out for flat knitting:

-Rows 1-3: Purl 4, knit 4, purl 4, knit 4, purl 4

-Row 4: Purl 4, cl2, purl 4, cl2, purl 4

-Row 5-7: Purl 4, knit 4, purl 4, knit 4, purl 4

-Row 8: Purl 4, cl2, purl 4, cl2, purl 4

BRAIDS

Braids, like other more complex cables, are made up of the same basic cable right and cable left cables. When completed, a braided cable looks like a three-strand braid. The cable stitches will not be aligned in your work.

Charted, a braided cable looks like this:

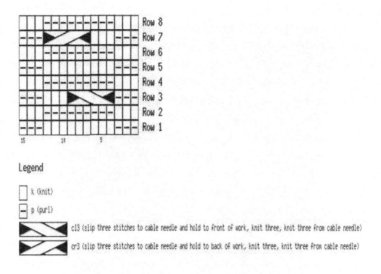

Legend

☐ k (knit)

⊟ p (purl)

▧ cl3 (slip three stitches to cable needle and hold to front of work, knit three, knit three from cable needle)

▧ cr3 (slip three stitches to cable needle and hold to back of work, knit three, knit three from cable needle)

Written out for flat knitting:

Braided cable, worked over 15 stitches and 8 rows, looks like this:

-Rows 1 and 5 (RS): P3, k9, p3

-Rows 2, 4, 6, and 8: K3, p9, k3

-Row 3: P3, cl3, k3, p3

-Row 7: P3, k3, cr3, p3

KNOTS

The same basic cables can form knots that look quite complex, even if they're really relatively simple. Some knitted cables are relatively dense, while others may intertwine in a more complex way. Work this knot over a multiple of 4 stitches + 6 stitches, for instance, 30 stitches.

This is a simple cable knot chart:

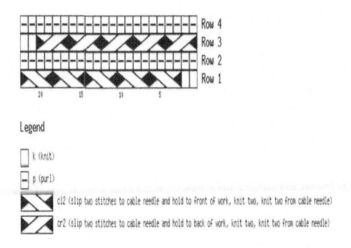

Legend

☐ k (knit)

⊟ p (purl)

◼◻ cl2 (slip two stitches to cable needle and hold to front of work, knit two, knit two from cable needle)

◻◼ cr2 (slip two stitches to cable needle and hold to back of work, knit two, knit two from cable needle)

Written out for flat knitting:

-Row 1 (RS): k2, *Cl2, repeat from * to end

-Row 2 and 4: Purl

-Row 3: *Cr2, repeat to last 2 stitches, K2

XO CABLES

Sometimes called the hugs and kisses cable, the XO cable is a pattern consisting of the letters X and O. The cable is worked over 20 stitches and 16 rows, but can be repeated as many times as needed.

The XO cable is charted as follows:

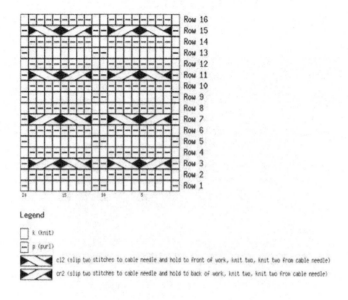

Legend

☐ k (knit)

⊟ p (purl)

◤◥ cl2 (slip two stitches to cable needle and hold to front of work, knit two, knit two from cable needle)

◢◣ cr2 (slip two stitches to cable needle and hold to back of work, knit two, knit two from cable needle)

Written out for flat knitting:

-Rows 1, 5, 9 and 13: *P1, k8, p1; repeat from * to end

-Row 2 and all WS rows: *K1, p8, k1; repeat from * to end

-Rows 3 and 7: *P1, cr2, cl2, p2, cl2, cr2, p1; repeat from * to end

-Rows 11 and 15: *P1, cl2, cr2, p2, cr2, cl2, p1; repeat from * to end

-Row 16: Repeat row 2

-Repeat rows: 1–16

CHAPTER 8: LACE PATTERNS

SIMPLE EYELETS

You can create a row of simple eyelets in any knitting pattern. An eyelet row adds an accent, while a single eyelet can be used for a simple buttonhole.

Written out for flat knitting:

-Row 1: Knit

-Row 2: Purl

-Row 3: Knit

-Row 4: Purl

-Row 5: K1, *yo, k2tog, repeat from * to one stitch from end, k1

DIAGONAL EYELETS

Diagonal eyelet patterns can be used for scarves, dishcloths or even socks and sweaters.

This is a very simple eyelet pattern and a good introduction to lace knitting.

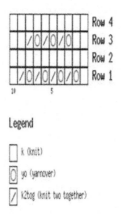

Legend

☐ k (knit)

☐ yo (yarnover)

☐ k2tog (knit two together)

-Row 1 (WS): K1, *yo, K2 tog, repeat from * to last stitch, K1

-Row 2: Knit

-Row 3: K2, *yo, K2 tog, repeat from * until 2 st remain, K2

-Row 4: Knit

ZIG ZAG LACE

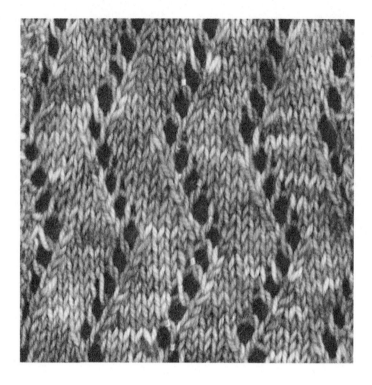

Zig zag lace creates vertical zig zags, ideal for scarves, socks and other projects. This is somewhat harder than the above lace patterns, but it's still quite easy to follow and produces a pretty and delicate appearance.

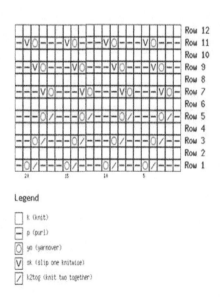

Legend

☐ k (knit)

☐ p (purl)

☐ yo (yarnover)

☐ sk (slip one knitwise)

☐ k2tog (knit two together)

Written out for flat knitting:

-Row 1 (WS): * P3, k2tog, yo; repeat from * to last stitch, p1

-Row 2 and all RS rows: Knit

-Row 3: P2, * k2tog, yo, p3; repeat from * to last 4 stitches, k2tog, Yo, p2

-Row 5: P1, * k2tog, yo, p3; repeat from * to end

-Row 7: P1, * yo, sl 1, k1, psso, p3; repeat from * to end

-Row 9: P2, * yo, sl 1, k1, psso, p3; repeat from * to last 4 stitches, Yo, sl 1, k1, psso, p2

-Row 11: P3, * yo, sl 1, k1, psso, p3; repeat from * to last 3 stitches, Yo, sl 1, k1, psso

SHELL LACE

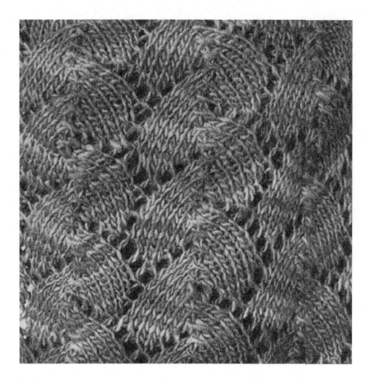

Shell lace creates a series of rounded, overlapping shapes, marked and surrounded by eyelets. This pattern can be used for socks or scarves, but can also be worked into curved shawls and other patterns. Work over a multiple of 11 stitches + 1.

Charted Shell Lace pattern:

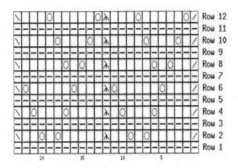

Row 12
Row 11
Row 10
Row 9
Row 8
Row 7
Row 6
Row 5
Row 4
Row 3
Row 2
Row 1

Legend

☐ k (knit)

⊟ p (purl)

◯ yo (yarnover)

◥ ssk (slip, slip knit)

◢ k2tog (knit two together)

◮ sk2p (slip one, knit two together, pass slipped stitch over)

Written out for flat knitting:

-Row 1 (WS) and all WS Rows: Purl

-Row 2: k2tog, *k5, yo, k1, yo, k2, sl 1, k2tog, psso; repeat from *, end last repeat ssk instead of sl 1, k2tog, psso

-Row 4: k2tog, *k4, yo, k3, yo, k1, sl 1, k2tog, psso; repeat from *, end last repeat ssk instead of sl 1, k2tog, psso

-Row 6: k2tog, *k3, yo, k5, yo, sl 1, k2tog, psso; repeat from *, end last repeat ssk instead of sl 1, k2tog, psso

-Row 8: k2tog, *k2, yo, k1, yo, k5, sl 1, k2tog, psso; repeat from *, end last repeat ssk instead of sl 1, k2tog, psso

-Row 10: k2tog, *k1, yo, k3, yo, k4, sl 1, k2tog, psso; repeat from *, end last repeat ssk instead of sl 1, k2tog, psso

-Row 12: k2tog, * yo, k5, yo, k3, sl 1, k2tog, psso; repeat from *, end last repeat ssk instead of sl 1, k2tog, psso

CHEVRON LACE

While zig zag lace creates a vertical zig zag, chevrons run horizontally across your knitting. Like the zig zag pattern, this is a rather easy lace pattern and good practice for more complex designs. Work over any multiple of 10 stitches + 1 stitch.

Charted Chevron Lace:

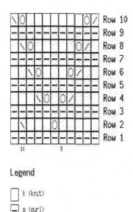

Legend

☐ k (knit)

⊟ p (purl)

Ⓞ yo (yarnover)

◩ ssk (slip, slip knit)

◪ k2tog (knit two together)

Written out for flat knitting:

-Row 1 (wrong side) and all wrong side rows: Purl.

-Row 2: *knit 5, ssk, knit 3. Repeat from * across, end with a knit 1.

-Row 4: *Knit 3, k2tog, yo, knit 1, yo, ssk, knit 2. Repeat from * across, end knit 1.

-Row 6: *Knit 2, k2tog, yo, knit 3, yo, ssk, knit 1. Repeat form * across, end knit 1.

-Row 8: *Knit 1, k2tog, yo, knit 5, yo, ssk. Repeat form * across, end knit 1.

-Row 10: k2tog, yo, knit 7, *yo, slip 1, k2tog, PSSO, yo, knit 7. Repeat from * across, end yo, ssk.

-Repeat these 10 rows for pattern.

FEATHER AND FAN

Feather and fan is a traditional lace pattern that works well for shawls, blankets and baby blankets. While it is a relatively long repeat, it's easily memorized and produces a lovely fluid fabric. Work in repeats of at least 24 stitches.

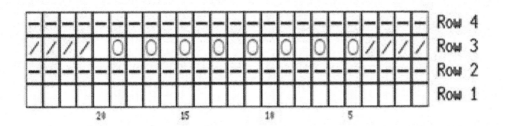

−	−	−	−	−	−	−	−	−	−	−	−	−	−	−	−	−	−	−	−	−	−	−	Row 4
/	/	/	/		O		O		O		O		O		O		O		O	/	/	/	/	Row 3
−	−	−	−	−	−	−	−	−	−	−	−	−	−	−	−	−	−	−	−	−	−	−	Row 2
																							Row 1

Legend

☐ k (knit)

⊟ p (purl)

⊡ yo (yarnover)

⬦ k2tog (knit two together)

Written out for flat knitting:

-Row 1: (RS) Knit

-Rows 2 and 4: Purl

-Row 3: *k2tog 4 times, yo, k1 8 times, k2tog 4 times; repeat from * to end

-Rep rows 1–4

FEATHER LACE STITCH

Feather lace is another option for a wide range of projects. Well-blocked, this lace stitch can look quite impressive; however, it's a simple 4-row repeat.

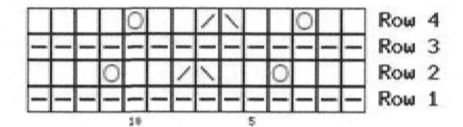

Written out for flat knitting:

-Row 1 and 3 (WS): Purl

-Row 2: K3, *yo, k2, ssk, k2tog, k2, yo, k1; repeat from * to last 2 st, K2

-Row 4: K2, *yo, k2, ssk, k2tog, k2, yo, k1; repeat from* to last 3 st, end with K3 instead of K1

...And Knit!

Keep in mind that this is simply an introduction to knitting stitches. With time and practice, you'll find you can move well beyond this beginner stitch dictionary, integrate various stitches into your projects and explore more complex knitting of all types. You'll be ready to move on once you've mastered both gauge and charts. The next chapter is a more in depth knitting terms glossary.

CHAPTER 9: GLOSSARY

Here is a list of the abbreviations and their meanings used in the preceding patterns. These are commonly used in most knitting patterns, as well.

k – knit

p – purl

sl – slip

st – stitch

k2tog – knit 2 together

k2tog tbl – knit 2 together through the back loops

ssk – slip, slip, knit

skp – slip 1, knit 1, pass slipped stitch over the knit stitch and off the needle

s2kp – slip 2 stitches (one at a time) to right needle, knit 1, pass 2 slipped stitches over the knit stitch and off the needle.

sl1-k2tog-psso – slip 1, knit 2 together, then pass slipped stitch over.

M1L – make 1 left

M1R – make 1 right

yo – yarn over

RS – right side

WS – wrong side

wyib – with yarn in back; the working yarn is held to the back of the work while the stitch (often a slip stitch) is worked

wyif – with yarn in front; the working yarn is held to the front of the work while the stitch (often a slip stitch) is worked

C4F – Slip 2 stitches to cable needle and hold in front, knit 2 from left needle, knit 2 from cable needle.

C4B – Slip 2 stitches to cable needle and hold in back, knit 2 from left needle, knit 2 from cable needle.

C6F – Slip 3 stitches to cable needle and hold in front, knit 3 from left needle, knit 3 from cable needle.

C6B – Slip 3 stitches to cable needle and hold in back, knit 3 from left needle, knit 3 from cable needle.

2/1 RPC– Slip 1 to cable needle and hold in back, knit 2 from left needle, purl 1 from cable needle.

2/1 LPC– Slip 2 to cable needle and hold in front, purl 1 from left needle, knit 2 from cable needle.

1/1 RPC– Slip 1 to cable needle and hold in back, knit 1 from left needle, purl 1 from cable needle.

1/1 LPC– Slip 1 to cable needle and hold in front, purl 1 from left needle, knit 1 from cable needle.

MC – main color

CC – contrasting color

Printed in Great Britain
by Amazon

36892030R00053